About the Author

Carla Baudin is a Norfolk-born author who predominantly writes literature on mental health. She completed a BA in English, moving on to study an MA in Twenty-First Century Literature at the University of Lincoln, and now writes full time as well as being a new mother to a son, Eli.

Voices in the Dark

Carla Baudin

Voices in the Dark

Olympia Publishers

London

www.olympiapublishers.com
OLYMPIA PAPERBACK EDITION

A CIP catalogue record for this title is
available from the British Library.

ISBN: 978-1-78830-147-3

First Published in 2018

Olympia Publishers
60 Cannon Street
London
EC4N 6NP

Printed in Great Britain

Dedication

To my parents, who never gave up on me.

Acknowledgments

For Everyone,
Who has ever struggled,
Ever supported,
Ever cared.

Foreword

Voices in the Dark is an autobiographical account of depression, anxiety, and psychosis. It was written during a period of deep depression, and can be very overwhelming and dark to read. Its journey through Admittance, Acceptance and Emergence can be at times bleak and overpoweringly desperate, somewhat harrowing for loved ones and carers to read; yet it is important that the true feelings of depression are narrated in all their forms, to give others a deeper understanding of the spiral that is mental illness and the merry-go-round-like fashion in which it manifests itself, on the long journey to recovery.

This book was written over a full year, bookended by two hospital admissions and four Accident and Emergency admissions throughout. It is therefore written with a sense of my feelings at the time; these do not reflect my current mental state, although they do accurately reflect the difficult and sometimes seemingly impossible road to recovery. However, as you move through the book from Admittance, Acceptance towards Emergence you will feel a shift in tone from that of more isolated misery, suicidal ideation and self-harm behaviours, to more positive and open-minded perspectives. It is as though you are staring down a deep dark hole and slowly, as you climb, you will see the light emerge. This is depression at its most raw, and, however difficult, it must be faced with understanding and compassion by all of us, as individuals and as a community.

It is something which many of us will face in our lifetimes, to varying degrees, and something that all of us will encounter through loved ones, or colleagues, neighbours or friends, however well hidden. The book is therefore to open up conversation about mental health, to ask the reader to immerse themselves in this world, and to question how they can help and influence change; to offer comfort to those reading and suffering, to let them know that they are not alone in their feelings, and to offer some hope, in that, eventually, things will change.

Although the book can be read as bleak, it is also a call for action, and one for believing in systems and in recovery. It is as it were an overview of the multi-faceted nature of mental illness, as well as a deeply personal journey. I was lucky enough to receive help through therapy and care systems, and to have a supportive family standing by; but recovery is possible for everyone, regardless of your situation, and will eventually lead to a new way of living with your condition, not by it. For me, this meant a reinvention of myself, to break away from this past depression and move forward with my life; it meant a change in the way I saw myself, and the world around m; and the opportunity to become a mother changed my life completely. Sometimes it takes something small to witness a change, sometimes it is much larger, but this book is one of triumph, to stand now recovered and well and look back and reflect on those memories and times, to which I can now no longer truly relate.

For those suffering my words would be, "have faith;" faith in the care systems, in those put in charge of helping, of those who offer an open ear and kind heart, and make the most of every opportunity to make yourself feel something more than your depression. For those who are carers, I hope this book offers some insight, however difficult, to allow you to ponder and question how to help; in most cases, that is simply to be open, honest, loving and kind.

The best way to read this book is therefore in its entirety from beginning to end, or sporadically, choosing a section which you feel best reflects where you are at with your illness, or picking poems throughout at random to grasp an overview of the tone of the book and the tumultuous nature of mental illness. My next endeavour is to write a more positive and bright collection of poetry, to assist in aiding people's recovery and highlighting the stories of others who have now finished their journey. Details can be found at the back of the book.

For those who wish to read on, I thank you for undertaking this journey with me, and I hope it brings you a better understanding of the nature of mental illness.

Carla Baudin

Thank you

For all those who left
When I was in tatters, broken, bereft
When I needed them, when I needed you
To support me, just to see me through
As I would have done for all of you
So-called friends, only on calm shores
To the partners, who hit and beat
Raised a hand 'til I was quiet, incomplete
To those that violated my self, my dignity
To all those that said they loved me, unconditionally
To the doctors who ignored,
The care co-ordinators too busy, my existence obscured

Thank you
For giving me the strength
To fight on, to find some wealth
Of self-sustainability and get the right help
To find me in this fractured and bruised self
To allow me to have the courage to acknowledge
Be honest and open, my personal promise,
To meet people, friends who really cherish
The nurses who really looked after me, unselfish

The family that never gave up on me
And always accepted me for me
To guide and support, 'til I found my place
And built a life to treasure and embrace.

Time

Three hundred and sixty-five days a year
Three hundred and sixty-five full of cheer
Three hundred and sixty-five to hold clear
So why are mine so full of fear?

Twelve months, just fifty-two weeks
Twelve months to fulfil what your heart seeks
Twelve months to climb life's milestone peaks
So why has mine left me vulnerable and weak?

Twenty-four hours in a day
Twenty-four hours to make, enjoy your way
Twenty-four hours to embrace come what may
So why are mine so full of hurt and pain?

Sixty minutes in an hour
Sixty minutes to feel empowered
Sixty minutes to change, grow, flower
So why are mine fought encased in armour?

Every second is a new
Every second a different view

Every second a choice by you
So what are mine so tainted blue?

Each date or day a memory
Of abuse of pain, never set free
Each date a chance to reflect on me
So why when I'm done am I punished to be?

Surreal

Everything is a bit surreal
All too much to really deal
Sat with family discussing house plans
When I've lost everything, my job, my home, my man

Life's in boxes scattered around
A shattered mirror on the ground
The reality of my life has set in
My resolve worn paper-thin

Sorting, sifting through piles of clothes
Reminding me of the vessel I loathe
Moving back to this place called home
This pattern in life somehow set in stone

Feeling like a constant failure
Always at risk, always in danger
No cry for help or intention unclear
Ready to go without resistance or fear

It's all been too much to bear and face
The end to torment I readily embrace

Since my adolescence, my teenage years
I've remained broken but no tears

No more sorrow or anger to part
Just the overwhelming need to depart
It's finally come, it's finally my time
The last unrelenting sign.

Settled no longer in turmoil
No one's lives will I continue to spoil
I've got my way, I've done my best
Finally now, my chance to rest.

Calm

Today is a day of calm,
Off to sleep, never to see the sun
I've made my decision, I've my way out
And in my mind is no hesitation or doubt

Break the seal foil, count them all
Hundreds of tablets, each one so small
But all together they've the power and might
To finally end my torturous fight

I say goodbye to Mum and Dad
Tell them I love them, difficult and sad
For in a few hours it'll be tomorrow
And I'll have left them bereft with sorrow

How much to prepare, do I leave a note?
Even though it won't explain, whatever I wrote
Do I move my savings, write my will?
No, I think this time I'll leave it still

Today at home I felt misplaced
Home has never felt in a safe place

But now despite everything I'm sitting smiling
For after this, I'll now need to keep trying

Each choking handful feels like a reprieve
From everything that has happened to me.
I know it's backwards, but I know it's true
Even though I'll miss everyone and always love you

Now to sleep, to rest my heavy head
Never to wake from this cosy little bed.

Setback

Now I am left completely confined
Self-harm and panic attacks, myself I resign
Already been struggling to keep safe,
Now with no grounding or sturdy base
Expectations to get on and keep up strength
Keep moving forward, just another day's length
Such a long few days though
When friends are together as if they don't know
I am out of sight and out of mind
Something to forget, everything's fine

I know it doesn't all go back to one event
But with so much history to resent
That came to pass years ahead
Leaving the broken abused, feeling dead
Today the head's so loud, won't shut up
Give up, get out, and continue to cut
Don't eat, too fat, no sleep, no rest
Just put an end to life's test

Why keep fighting on your own
No-one can support, whoever you phone

Might as well accept, it is what it is
And you have tried and failed, in all of this
Swinging, pushing, ever a lost cause
No-one ever considering you, even a second's pause
No consideration of the 'you' in the midst
Of all the discomfort, in pain that won't desist

So might as well wave goodbye
Give up and work on the grim reaper scythe.

Aftermath

Waking up with blood on my face
I can't see anything, I feel so spaced
I cannot walk or feel my hands
To the bathroom, lock the door, this isn't as planned.
There stands Mum, all a blur,
Is she really there, standing by the door?
"Ambulance is coming, hang on in there!"
This isn't what I wanted, this isn't fair.

My throat is burning, my head's a mess
I can't make out anything, it's all go, stress
Doctors, nurses, travelling on blue lights
I wasn't meant to make it through the night
An hour they say is all I've got
Maybe this time I've hit the spot
The nurse attending, so beautiful, an angel to me
I ask her to let me go, finally set me free.

But no one listens, presume it's the drugs
Then everything, organs, start to pick up
From dialysis and transplants to no longer critical
Through the worst but still very ill

I can't make sense, I can't compute
This world is hazy, everything on mute
The only thing I can hear is that
"No point us all sitting watching, fact".

I'm made more stable, pumped full of meds,
Discharged from rhesus to an acute bed
Surrounded by people genuinely ill
And me, only in here by my own will
I'll admit it's humbling, hard to take
That this situation was all for my sake
I wasn't meant to be wasting everyone's time
Hooked up to twenty-four-hour IV lines

Saving my life minute by minute,
Feeling bad that parents had to see it.
Apart from that, I feel completely numb
How am I still here? Emotionally stunned
Coming to terms with still being alive
When you were ready, heart set, to die
They keep me on observations, hourly bloods
Family all there with concerned looks and hugs

All I want is to get out, relax and slip out
See the doctor, "No long term harm or damage"
A miracle they say, they should soothe but I feel panic
How am I going to complete this again?
When everyone will be on high alert, tight reins

I still don't understand why I'm being punished
I'd had enough and thought this time I'd done it.

Confused

Back home is too surreal
I still can't equate or begin to feel
Everyone else is striving on
Acting like nothing is at all wrong

Changing phone numbers and addresses
They think they're helping clean up my messes
But there I sit all bemused
I shouldn't be here, I'm so confused

Everyone is tense, I can see they can't cope
They see it in my eyes, there is no hope
I watch them cry and break down
And all I want is to be underground

They're sending in the crisis teams
To see how I am, how I've been
As though they could do anything to help
When I've given up and hate myself

They support a hospital admission
And I know it's not really my decision

So I'll go, try to keep them happy,
And act as though it'll work, this therapy.

I sit, I talk but none of it's real
I'm disassociated, locked in by a tight seal
But off I'll be packed to a psychiatric ward
With some desperate hope of moving forward

But now I know it's a waste of time
I'm too far gone down the line
They'll assess me, new meds then it'll all pause
Until they give up and realise I'm a lost cause.

Section

So suddenly I'm here, within a few hours,
From a phone call to an ambulance
Into medical power, they strip me of anything
That can cause me harm
But I know I'll find a way, so stand still, so calm

People screaming, drifting aimlessly about
Playing games, sitting, staring out
How did I end up in a place like this?
Is my mind really stuck, or something to be fixed?

After all these years, I know it's fucked
It's just a matter of time before they all give up
They'll get fed up of bleeding wrists
Of choking attempts, myself a constant risk

So instead I'll be on twenty-four-hour observation
To stop any further devastation.
Someone following me around everywhere they said
Someone sat through the night at the end of my bed

I'll ask to leave after all I'm voluntary

But suddenly under section, here I'll be
Twenty-eight days at least the stay
Wasting time drawing, writing, talking through each day
What a waste of everyone's time
I've already come to the end of the line

Assessments

So your name is x, and your condition is y
Not that that's important, that's by the by
What we want to do, is find out what we can do for you
You struggle each and every day, in getting on with tasks you say
Washing, bathing is the same too, staring at your stretched,
scarred skin it's true
Dressing must be much the same, squeezing your clothes on to
your average frame
Eating you say is also a problem, from prepping to organising to
devouring, troublesome
You are visibly shaking, are you okay? Could you have got here,
made your own way?
Remembered all that you had to say, about your difficulties each
and every day
Would you have been able to cope, without support from your
friends and hope?
Well here is how I see things, so, an eating disorder at your weight,
no,
You didn't present deafness in the perfectly quiet waiting room,
You attended, arrived chaperoned, so no demons to loom
You spoke, engaged and talked honestly
With no emotion, no break in voice, no hint of pain in your reality

You've scratched and nipped, and hurt yourself but I believe you've
a clean bill of mental health
No need for government guideline tests, to see if you're ill,
deranged or depressed
For me it's easy to decide, no further help do you require
Your condition portrays you as a liar.

Safe Place

I found myself a new haven, my safe place
In the corner, squashed in a small space
Tucked away, cowering, shrinking still
Away from patients, doctors, pills
My voice's craze shouting to give up
Everything feels all too much
I cannot think, see or feel,
I still feel dead, lifeless, unreal

We get knocked for breakfast, lunch and tea
And meds prescribed in-between
It's all a very strange routine
After everything, that past that's been
I still can't shower or get undressed
Even being here, puts agoraphobia to the test

I make everyone's lives so much worse
Like some bad smell or lingering curse
None of them will even come to see,
They'd all be better off without me
Without the concern and constant blame,
The hopeless feelings that always remain

Is it too much to ask to take your life
Still they stop me, try as I might
They're punishing me by keeping me here
With flashbacks and voices in my ear

Just let me go
Let me die
Let me have
My last goodbye.

Acceptance

Tears and fears constantly relived
More pills, more days, my mind a sieve
Up I sit, wide awake
With movies and painful memories
Beating, punishing myself 'til I bleed
I have never felt so depressingly alone
Even like this when I'm at home
The nurses are lovely and talk to us lots
About your issues, problems to sort
They genuinely seem to care for us
They try to build friendships, comfort and such
The best thing I've found is total distraction
Talking to others, my front well practised
They seem to all rush to open up to me
And that gives me a break from anything I see
Some seem normal, some seem calm,
They all seem nice, un-judgemental, no harm
Then there's a few lovely people too
In here each connection is so real, so true
Not like outside with social expectation
Or conforming to life's social conventions
Everyone is just left to be
Whatever they feel, completely free.

Birthday

It might be my birthday but it's no time to celebrate
I find myself in melancholy, unable to relate
Family visit with gifts and all
And all I want to do is collapse on the floor

It's all too much, trying to be OK
Pretend they know what to say
When we all sit completely lost
And they try to console me and touch me so soft
As though I'm fragile and might just break
Or somehow I'll lose my last sane slate

I can't even accept presents, what to say
When life I reject, each and every day
They try their hardest, do their best
But I can see it's putting everything under duress

I'm exhausted, lost, not really there,
Yet surrounded by people that love and care
They say they love me, try to keep safe,
I want to scream, "Let me die, leave this place"
Nothing will cut through the pain
When every day I'm forced to remain.

Hear it say

They've moved my room for what purpose I can't see
Why can't I just be left alone to be?
Instead now I'm right up the hall,
Where I can hear the office phone calls
Everyone walking constantly on the floor
The meds aren't working, I can't see why
"They should be, keep giving them a try"
"Its fine, we can always change them again,
Get you back on the mend"
I'm still suicidal every day, I'll admit
I think I'll always feel this way; it won't quit
My voices remain, so, so loud
They aren't ever drowned out by the crowds
Hear me now, for I will pray,
End this life, I hear it say.

Tomorrow

Another attempt, hanging the same
With some twine, I was given again
This can't fail, I have no doubt,
Nothing left to say or talk about

Five hours later, I open my eyes
All these minutes have gone by
I cannot see, barely breathe,
Bloodshot eyes and purple, yet no reprieve

My face is blue, neck swollen and black,
They took my observations, worried how to react
But soon as ever I'm back and fine,
Even though I was close to the line,

I go to smoke and sit in the rain,
Laughing through my wretched pain,
Why me, why are you keeping me here,
I sit and cry, but not a single tear

Now once again, they've raided my room,
Taken away my pieces, but still soon
I'll have some more, a smashed cup,
It'll do the trick, it will be sharp.

Stalked

Followed around, one-to-ones,
Because you've put yourself in grievous harm
With cuts so deep they're all worried
And I'm supposed to feel bad, feel sorry
For causing my loved ones so much concern
With cuts and ligatures and a fair few burns
Why the hassle traipsing with me around
When I'm berated by so many sounds
They don't seem to realise how much pain
There's only so much suffering someone can sustain
No section for my intelligence and capacity
To know if they'll set me free
I'll go and die, finish this life off
And no one, no care will make me stop
Determined, stubborn they might say
But I will have my end, next week, or now
I've got my plan I even know how
I'll have my end eventually
One day they'll realise, in my death
They'll finally see.

Stuck

Stuck, stuck in the mud,
Nowhere to run
Nowhere to hide
The voices get louder
Deep inside
Get out, give up
It's time to die

Stuck, stuck in darkness
No light to guide,
No hope to find
It seeps, pulses, poisons
My insides
Get out, give up
No tears to cry

Stuck, stuck, stuck in this self
No place of comfort
Nowhere to escape
Trapped in this body
This being I loathe,
Get out, give up

The defeating sigh

Stuck, stuck, stuck with a past forgot
No solace found
No progress, no ground
Haunted by abuse and pain
Memories all still the same
Get out, give up
It's all too much

Stuck, stuck, stuck with myself
No love, no self-worth
No chance of rebirth
Formed and frayed in this place
For rest, for sleep, I'll pray
Get out, give up
My final try.

The Lie

I can't handle people saying they see the best in me
The lie, this person, I present to be,
The truth, it seeps, it tears apart
It poisons my head and blackens my heart
Beauty, love, kindness and care
These words choke or further ensnare
They say I won't see the goodness in me
But they don't see or share the voices that be
Lust, disgust, abused and dead
Forever thoughts of self-harm
Self-loathing in my head,
Why the world won't let me be
I wish that someone would just see
I write, I colour, I talk, I draw
Covering up this deep inherent flaw
This broken child, a cracked porcelain doll
Haunted by the knell of deaths, never-ending toll.

Left

They're all getting out, leaving me behind
To rot in self-loathing, in darkness so blind
Two of the best went yesterday
The next week, my insides fester
Their outlook sunny, mine for ever bleak
People text, try to reach out, sending love and wishes of health
Words and lies, they try to spout
Lost, torn, self-hating self
Today I've got my review, medications, diagnosis, treatment plans
They promise dieticians, programmes renewed
The supposed supported, outreached mental-health hand
Hospitals or prisons keeping you alive
I'll stay I'll try until my last
When, finally, I get my great goodbye.

Beaten

Beat, hit, bruise me more,
Screaming, crying on the floor,
Wailing, locked up so many doors,
Feeling the echoes of pains gone before

Slice, cut, bleed me again
Yet still the pain always remains
When our last strength can't be regained
And every day still stays the same

Hate, loathe, leave me behind
No nurse or loved one could be so kind
The only thing real, the pain I feel
The bodily hurt shows my self-worth

For you see what was done to me
This body damaged, self-taken from me
Abuse and pain is all I know
Smack, punch, have another go

Slam, flat, forehead into wall,
No deeper can I ever fall

Punish, patience, punish me again
From this self-torture I'll never refrain

Make it physical, it's all I know
Until that final deafening blow.

Acting Up

I don't feel I can be myself
Or they'll turn around and pull their help
No tear, no drama, no depth of despair,
Can't talk, can't reach out or even share

Those thoughts and feelings we keep within,
Or moments we lost it all, just give in,
I think they'll ship me out, write me off
Like a truly lost cause, they'll have had enough

When I'm starting to feel like I've a place in this world
Everything seems to unravel, unfurl,
When finally I'm feeling safe and ready to try
Like the world will give up, leave me to die.

I've been trying so far as hard as I can,
To open up, except help, take the professionals' hand
But now it feels threatened, like I'm "acting up"
Like no one really understands, no one gives a fuck

Maybe, finally I've lost the plot and this really is my lot
Everything today seems so confused and I'm lost, bemused

Am I past help, am I really that bad?
Has my reality warped, am I really mad?

Has my logic and sense really started to blur,
To be honest, today, I can't be sure
Tomorrow I'll try to regroup and rest
And tackle each challenge and do my best

For somewhere, somehow there must be hope
A way to manage to live and cope
Thoughts whir and muddle inside my mind

Maybe I'm not supposed to be alive?
Despite the wanting, thoughts and feelings,
Maybe there's a way of repairing, healing?

Care

Don't say you care when you stand and stare, while the pained
scream, living their nightmare dream
Don't say you give a damn, when you won't lend a helping hand,
To those desperately in need, so full of anguish they bleed
Don't say you understand, when you withhold help because you
can,
When you discharge those you don't understand, to home, to
others themselves, to harm
Don't say you're all near, when we beat ourselves and you can hear
You stay outside far away, leaving us alone in our dark day
Don't say you're here to talk, yet hear us wail helplessly inside, yet
in corridors you stand and hide
Don't stand with a fake smile and kid yourselves all the while,
That you're really here for us, when your actions show your words
are dust.

Crumb

Hide your face from the light
Don't be afraid of this delight
It's only a nice little treat
That I know your brain does seek
Just take a little taste
It would be rude just to waste
And yet you know that even a crumb
Will wend its way to your hips, your bum
You'll watch as your face begins to bloat
And in your misery your disorder will gloat
You'll watch as your body begins to swell
As the mirror will only tell
Everyone will see your glutinous want
And your reflection your mind will haunt

Walls

I am here
I can see the writing on the walls
And hear the screams from rooms down the hall
And feel the sense of growing fear
But still, I am here

I see the monopoly board
And the patients on the ward
Trying to be here
Though I feel back there
Though I am not alive and there is nowhere to hide

I try to understand the psychiatrist
Though their words my brain does resist
I see the bars and gates that hold me in
So I am here
Although I'm dead within

I hear the laughter and feel the tears
Living this prolonged nightmare
When your lot in life hasn't been fair
I'll try to keep hope, clear
For better for worse, for now
I am here.

Art

Paint colour, draw and see
A mind displaced, blurred in a page, set free
It's all art therapy, but it's mere distraction
From the demons that be
From all those thoughts, you cannot face
From that sense of loss, never replaced
Crying, shaking, frustratingly annoyed
Any emotion to fill the empty void

Conjure an image, pen it down
Shut the voices that constantly hound
The unsettling calm you try to drown,
That resolution found, decision made
Your life in tatters, but no longer afraid
That six feet under will be the proof
Your suicide being your happiest truth,
But draw and write and scribble away
Struggle through pencils and pastels
For just another day.

Cog

Just a cog trying to turn
So many spokes resist each move
How to spin a different way
So as not to repeat everlasting days

Just a cog, a wheel, a spoke
However hard I push, not enough fight
To make a change that will continue on
That will help me genuinely move on

Friends are leaving, everyone turns,
Losing my support, receiving such scorn
How to move forward and change this curse
Everything seems so much worse

One glimmer of hope, a tiny speck
Then return to reality and so much mess
Can't make change of my own accord
So how in life can I move forward?

I can't shower, change, before panic sets in
I see myself, the loathing, I look so grim

Even today one problem, just the wait
When there is so much to more debate

Agoraphobia, self equals self
I genuinely don't think I can be helped
Where to go, what to do,
I really think it's over, I'm through

Little normalities, a shattered dream
Back to reality with a crying scream
Housing, leaving, finding my own place,
The only thing safe in this "poppy" ward space

And then they'll just let me go
Whether I'm ready, or a risk to myself, I know
Hospitals helping, felt I was on the mend
Then perspective distorts, everything starts to bend

In here I live, a glimmer of hope
Out there I know I just can't cope
With even being, just to exist
Temptation everywhere too much to resist

They'll lift my section and I'll be gone
Cast out to a world I don't belong
They say there has to be a way
But I know it's in my dying day

I can't be forgiving but I can forget
And leave a past full of regret

Of blame and lack of responsibility
To allow myself the mind-set to be free

Cut my ties, cut myself off
To finally say I've had enough
To start anew, all unknown
And give me time to become and grow

Everything I know is all square
Everything I am, the people that care
I need to fit into a round hole,
Yet a square peg, the edges must be shaved and let go.

Trigger

Trigger dates coming my way, days before my release day
This place, the hospital is starting to work, but in those weeks my
mind's gone berserk
No way back, no way to cope, losing all of my hope
Suicidal, if I said, admission not helping
While mind and body are melting

How to explain, how I fear those days, could be the difference
between darkness and sun-rays
I can't help myself to figure this out, now anxiety and panic have
me in doubt
Let me stay, keep me safe, this responsibility I just can't take

Just let me get through and stay with reality, let me show you, so
you finally see
Refer me, defer me, find a new ward, somewhere, anywhere, here
or abroad
And again my life will be manageable, at least here I'm stable, this
progress not lost,

Or release me that week and I'll pay the ultimate cost

It's still too delicate, hope is thin, but at least on those days, this year I would win
But let me go before I'm ready, this solid ground I fear will be unsteady

The voices will become too loud and I'll be lost into darkness, that poisonousness, bottomless empty black cloud.

Playground

Up and down, a nightmare merry-go-round,
Everywhere risk, noise, threats surround
From all and any waking hours
Crowds, people, commonly I cower
How to re-introduce, re-integrate
Your life in words, your feelings you narrate
Locked, alone, hidden away
Keep shut off, here I'll stay
Family, friends, fiancé try to support
Still my head won't rest from retorts
You're useless, you're weak, you're not good enough
You're a failure, misery personified, constant dark.

Feel

Intellectualise, fine, I'll talk for hours
Of courses and voices and feelings that cower
Yet I can't make that connection
No emotion can ever be detected
Intelligence is such a weakness
Understanding everything, left with bleakness
But not to feel, to cry, to scream,
Makes me a nothing, an ongoing theme
That doctors and such think I'm doing well
Talking through my life, my private hell
Only to give up and finally say
There's nothing I can do, to help in any way
And so I'm left with all this knowledge
To impart, to share, to acknowledge
And yet it does me no good at all
And so each time, further I fall.

There

How can I leave and go back there, to all the people who say they
care
When nothing will they address, and everything is such a mess
Where everyone ignores the past, and replaces with the
pretence of the middle class
So now I'm stuck and can't return, to the so called safe haven
of "home"
But what are my options, going into the unknown, a women's
institute, a hostel all alone
Loved ones that can't understand, no one there to hold my
hand
With Christmas approaching, what a week, to be discharged,
tackle alone all that grief
But alone I would rather be, than have them discover, the
truth they'll see.
When I haven't even started on the issues, when hope, my
person is as delicate as wet tissue
Care co-ordinator, support plans, none of which will withstand
The hell that time will put me through, when I know I'm not
safe with myself in truth
The only way forward that I can see, is giving me the time to
be

When hospital is my only advance, we've exhausted every
avenue, my last chance

Move me, transfer me, a hospital, another ward, if it's about
patients or beds moving forward

Because I know I'm not ready to move forward, I'll end my life
by my own sword

Time is needed to find more strength, for all the talking,
trying to work through to create

The real me, despite the last hard few days, have been difficult,
I admit

But I've just got to find a way to use therapy and really
commit

I am trying so hard to keep me safe, however it's hard to be
open in this place

Finally seeing the light, glimmer inside, even if all in my life
try to deny and hide

How can I convince them it'll change at all, when doctors are
set on release, don't listen at all

Not being heard and ignored, placing my old behaviour in my
hands

Breaking my staff social rapport

Feeling a final sense of slight control,

From this mess that is my life my role

I guess I will soon find out, when they talk, discuss, reflect

And when I'm out into the "empty threats", but still at the
moment I believe I'm the defect

Even if things may be starting to shift

Most of the time my mind's at sea, adrift

I'll hope and pray they'll keep me somewhere

As only that scenario seems remotely fair

I guess I don't know what to say

But I live in hope that I'll have time to find my way.

Goal

Today's goal is all self-care,
Panic attacks, too much to bear
Regroup and rethink
Don't push too hard or go to the brink

Today's aim, not to hurt myself
Use the staff instead, ask for help
Shut myself off, for I've drained too much
With everything else, emails, texts and such

A day to focus just on me
To ground and gain some true reality
Try to ignore everything else,
Smell my perfumed stress ball, help myself

Reviews impending, will all can attend?
Hopefully by me some time to process, cement and mend
Fingers crossed, it'll all work out
Enough people on side to finally turn things about

Take control of my life and my release,
Save myself from pain and grief

Write down some stuff, let it out,
Close the book on dark thoughts and doubts

Still shaky and dizzy, try to rest
Don't do too much but still be busy
Sit and rest, me-time now
Shut the door, relax, have a lie down

I'm totally drained, too much spoken
Brain and synapses on misfire, broken
Feel like I need recovery to reconnect
To feelings that others can see

Today is hard, baby steps
Opening myself up, either ignore or reject
I'm gone, I'm done, I'm completely exhausted
At least it's down now, documented, reported.

Trying

Trying to keep myself safe,
Make the most of my stay in this place
I feel no help in each meeting
Assessing, questioning my soul, depleting
They're trying to put in place a support plan
To find some place of sturdier land

So even though everything's up in the air
There is a sense or attempt to show care
A time to be strong and take some solace
In the hope of help, a paper-thin promise
Hope my progress and support doesn't dwindle
To be lost again, left fragile and brittle

A tiny glimmer of calm
A grain of hope to hold in my palm
Something to cling to, something to help
Manage and rebuild this broken self
It may be weak, it may be small
But it may stop the collapse and further fall.

Thoughts turn to future goals and the like

And despite the goals that try as they might
For once, a second, I beat them down
A small victory found.

Discharge

When you leave hospital and they won't prescribe
All the meds you had inside
All that helped stabilise you to leave
A week is all that you'll receive
Then it's cold turkey, you're on your own
The seed of relapse already sewn
As before you couldn't cope
So how this time can you be expected to hope?
That you'll suddenly be alright
That each hour, each minute is less of a fight
When you know from past experience
That it doesn't work, half you, half meds, experienced
Setting you up for a fall
Leaving you waiting, pacing for that phone call
Of readmission to the place you came from
Section, hospital, it's all a con
The system fails you every time
Too much paperwork, tape and lines
It's all sad bullshit, so untrue
They don't think of patients, not about you
They're only concern is bed capacity
So you're left in crisis -
They just can't see.

Hope

My hope for this year is really quite simple
Find myself, be kind to myself, less critical
Be true, be honest and always fair
Show myself love, acceptance and self-care

Move away from the past and memories
Work through the pain and let them be
Learn to see the 'me' that's somewhere inside
No longer mourn the child lost, who needs to cry

Become the woman I am, that others all see
Drown the voices and set myself free
Grow, learn and always progress
Learn to relax and let go of stress

Claim my body, myself as my own
Conquer the noises that constantly drone
Gain back some independence, find my feet
Climb slowly out of this hovel so deep

Cover my scars with new tattoos
That represent positivity, not a life tainted blue

Mark myself in a positive way
Symbols to remind me each and every day.

Of the good and the new Carla I became
Walk into the light, no self-blame
No more punishment or self-hate
Instead a garden with buds and a village picturesque gate

No longer the victim, no longer the abused
No longer feeling I deserve to be used
To slowly gain confidence and sense of self worth
To reinvent myself, reborn in rebirth

To emerge like a butterfly from its cocoon
Find a life worth living, not one doomed
This year's challenge is to find me
Learn to accept what will be, will be.

Walking Dead

The Walking Dead ask for nothing but peace
From the pain and past, that final release
Existing, resisting, shuffling around
Burying heads in dreams six foot down
Not to a heaven or pearly gates
Just away from struggle and so much hate
From all those who deserve to be punished
Leave the caring, responsible, astonished
To take responsibility and blame
For letting everyone down and yet kept alive to remain
The Walking Dead, ever skulking about
Wishing for an attempt that works, to be found
Redemption or revenge isn't what we seek
Life ajar for even hope that bleak
All we want is some final rest
After all we've tried, we've done our best
We've carried it all and remained in silence
We're bored of scars and years of violence
By others, by us, by ourselves, by you
Our abuse is theirs but perpetuated by us too

The Walking Dead everlasting, yes, true

But we refuse to exist just for you
Let's stop the torture, the endless days,
We will go our soundless, separate ways.

Effort

Die and the pain goes away
Try and struggle, each and every day
Lie and everything remains the same
Cry and never mention who, what's to blame

Might, when there is nothing left to tend
Light, there is none in the end
Fight to find you're a lost cause
Night, everlasting sleep and pause

Deep rooted are our thoughts
Keep the voices, the words, the retort
Reap the benefits of silent demise
Leap into unknown dark skies.

Distract

Buy a car, do something else,
Anything to cover up how useless I felt
Make, remake, stab yourself, fail
Try to resist bingeing, to no avail

Paint toes, laugh, talk away
Waste the hours of the day
Laugh off the calm and hopeless feelings
Pretend it's okay, like you are only dreaming

Fix a pie and pastry,
Cook everyone a glorious tea,
Clean, clear and tidy away
Colour, write, keep your voices at bay

Can't accept you have no meds
Go have no sleep on top of your bed
Fight each urge, ligature up
Remove and berate, "you selfish fuck"

Never can win, never to defeat
Already battered, a body to beat

But smile and help and act okay
Try to convince, you, everyone, you may

That your coping moving forward,
As you sink with each hour
Skin scored

Dares

Who dares to care for those who share
Their deepest fears through unrelenting tears
As they break down, walls crashing to the ground
Their darkest thoughts laid bare,
Their eyes fixed in a numbing stare

I can't carry on replaying the same broken song
I just want it all to end, I'm past the point of any change of mind
I have these things in place, my exit plan,
This pain I can no longer stand

When you try your best to succeed
And it's impossible to get what you need
I've lost something I can't replace
My life is nothing, simply a waste

I'm ready to go, it's my time I know
Could you lend a helping hand, wrap their wounds in bandages?
Love and tell them to believe
In the help they might receive

Could you manage to talk them around?
When they're hell bent on six feet underground.

Pressure

So much pressure to carry on
From friends and family,
Loved ones all around
Striving on for their sake
When your last energy
Is every breath you take?

Others' lives, their futures in your hands
Basing their life on your plans
When what they ask you cannot offer
Knowingly heading, both to suffer
When they aren't showing you love
But you've already had enough

Our decision could be their downfall
Your wish, the last curtain call
Companions, lovers, family, friends
Promises made that won't relent
How to ask people to let you go
Live their lives without you, so

Roles are played, parts formed

Reality breaking with each dawn
Too much power, responsibility
How to let them go, set them free
Away from you, the damage your cause
Try to get through, personality on pause

Knowing everything they didn't see
Letting them know, to let things be
Self-destruction is one thing
How to make them see you're not their life
You struggle on your own
Not their fight or strife

Giving up, giving in to the voice within
Knowing you'll wreck so many lives
In your last final goodbye.

Pretty

Tell me I'm pretty, tell me I'm cute
Tell me I'm smart and kind and astute
Tell me I'm lovely, tell me I'm skinny
Tell me I'm soft and bones and skin
Tell me I'm precious, tell me I'm not fat
Tell me I'm respected and all of that
I won't hear the words you try to say
Won't see the way I brighten your day
Won't see how you stare at me
Won't see the future you want us to be
Won't see the smile when I'm near
Won't see anything but the fear
The fear you'll see through this façade
This confidence faked, in my regard
This happiness fraudulent in every smile
This feeling of stress rising all the while
All because you asked me to eat
Now internally I slump and weep
I see and hear nothing of the day
Just look for reassurance in some way
That I am attractive, that I am not fat
That I am something more than this act.

Stop

Stop laughing, giggling while our lives fall apart
Whilst we sit in stress and you discuss parties and dress
Christmas presents and festivities
While we sit crying, scared, trying to hide
Laughing like a hyena, cackle
When we've so many demons to tackle
You stand and talk amongst yourselves
But not to us even when we need your help
Sat talking across us all
As though we're invisible, not here at all
Such good people so full of care
Yet you smile and blankly stare
Not here for us but for a wage
To file some papers, complete a page
So carry on with your natter
Our voices will drown out your pointless chatter.

Cycles

Manage, derange, damaged, engage
Breathe, leave, cope, choke
Smile, revile, love, loathe
Fight, ignite, cut, stuck
Try, die, remember, defend
Eat, repeat, sick, quick
Silence, violence, awake, shake
Bleed, freed, stab, rehab
Meds, head, pills, will
Sleep, deep, next, rest
Swallow, follow, help, hurt
Bed, note written, dead

Scurry

Hurry, scurry, far away
Because this is the Walking Dead's Day
We've sobered up from all your pills
Seen through the fog with iron will

We're not alone, but strong together
Our madness will overthrow you forever
Because we may be deemed insane
But after what we witness, what remains

We know we're the ones full of heart
And you the ones that tear us apart
But not this day, yester-, tomorrow
No dwelling in strife and so much sorrow

We're here to say good morning, fuck you
Watch as we succeed and pull through
Get on top of our demons, one by one
Climbing higher and higher towards the sun

An army empowered, standing complete
Armour strong, impossible to defeat

It may take time, life's not fixed a day
But I swear to you we'll find a way

We'll slowly put all ills to right
And carve our own futures so bright

So screw you and the horse you rode in on
So this is our war cry, bring it on.

Ask

If I could ask for just one thing
It would be that hope isn't given so thin
So that it can never sustain
The past pressures, impossible to remain

Why keep offering these helping hands
When they crumble when touched, grains of sand
And slip through fingers that try to grip
A cruel, unfair, dishonest trick

Don't say it's all you can do
When we know that isn't true
When hope is only temporary
And so collapsed by memories

That loss of hope cuts so deep
That we've no more tears even to weep
We're left to all that's real
Unable to cope with how we feel

The only comfort we are ever left
Is knowing we hold our own death

So stop talking of endless possibilities
In clichés, dreams, new buds on trees

Because your metaphors are transparent, fake
And from us all pretend strength you'll take
As certainly you already know
So all I ask is for honesty you show

And for you all to let me be
Stop forcing me to stick around
When my place is underground
Stop telling me I can make a change
When past becomes present, becomes future remains

So if I could ask for just one thing
Let false hope go, let us give in.

Honest

How honest am I meant to be?
Talk from the heart, suicide all I see
Will that shut down some possibility
A way for change, a new way to be

Will my care-co even try to help?
Or leave me stranded, old addresses spelt
Already with a failing exit plan
Will they offer to make a stand?

To assist in setting myself up
With financial, care and housing support
Or is it just all going to be words
As I've experienced so far, all I know

There really is just one way forward
Except taking my life of my own accord
It all just seems like empty help
Managing for two weeks to cope

Move the problem, me, along
Put me away, from familiar to unknown

Anxiety too high, feeling stressed
Waking as ever panicked, depressed

Do I tell them about it all?
Repeat my history, all these notes from before
To make them understand all they've written
Who knows that's what's been put down?
Will they believe me or simply frown?

Accept me and let me stay
Or further reject me, each and every day
Who really knows if I've the capacity or choice?
I've still no decision, no options, no voice

Except for words scrawled on a page
Yet unread, just another stage.

More

The more you look, the more you see
What your life has come to be
Learned behaviours, belief systems deep
Feeling the only relief is never-ending sleep

Each relationship, situation you run through
Only compounds what you believe is true
The hand you've been dealt is far from fair
And you're alone, even though people say they care

Even things you thought okay
When talked about in the light of day
Suddenly appear the same, not right
Even more demons to sway and fight

So much history, where to start
Loving relationships that tore my soul apart
Supportive family with the best of intent
Only stifle and further cement

Reciprocal roles that cannot change
The damage that's done you can't rearrange

Going back so many years
Bringing nothing but re-liveable fears

Every session, more truth awakening
From the clouds of smoke you've hidden in
The belief, the you, you thought you knew
Smashed to dust, everything known untrue

Your basic principles, morals, understanding, love
Aren't anything like normal, all tarnished with mud
Where is the me in all this mess
What is the meaning of this life's cruel test?

Being pushed away, fighting rejection
Constant beration and unending dejection,
Now life in pieces on the floor
Staring at your mirrored self no more

Someone you don't recognise, someone who needs help
Except that person is still you, in hell
The one you've learnt to loathe and disapprove
Not able to stand being in your own body, you

No strength to save spirit, afraid of being seen
Each mark and scar disfiguring, a permanent bad dream
Self-hatred and punishment no longer suppressed
Separating you from before, more depressed

Punishing you, everything you deserve
No love in life, no cry heard

The voices repeating with never-ending din
Hating yourself, every speck, each inch of skin

When you're intelligent and can see it all
Articulate your feelings but not feel, you fall
Into a deeper painful state
Where you no longer feel, yet constantly awake

No wonder you feel like you can't withstand
The never-ending cycle of abuse at hands
Whether physical or mental, sexual or not
They've made you who you are, your confidence shot

Any hope in mind or body impossible
Neither are home and your actions unstoppable
No sleep offered for any solace
You try and try and swear and promise

You won't hurt yourself or overdose again
But that's like saying it'll never rain
You pray for something different tomorrow
Just to ease this perpetuating sorrow.

If self equals self, how can you move on?
This is my reality, my broken song.

System

How can things work out right?
When it's the system you're trying to fight
To get the support you need to move on
And not return to the place you're least strong
Where people don't listen or understand
Where you're not safe, no one around
When what you need is a settled place
A tiny corner of sanity for recovery, a space

Away from troubles but with professionals there
To help support with treatment and care
Everything's a fine balancing act
Not to end up at the start, ten steps back
Is it really so much to ask?
To do the right thing by patients and trust
That we know our situation better than anyone else
We know what will help, what we need for ourselves

Who knows what to do or what to say?
A normal mental health patient's day.

Nightmare

Day nightmares, living without prayer
Sitting empty inside, that blank, 'I'm fine' stare
Try to distract, block them out
But they always remain, always about
Left to be, to struggle all alone
Never really feeling at home
Stuck in a mind that doesn't belong
Shackled in darkness, forever, lifelong.

See

I see them all, every face,
All those loved, all those disgraced
I see them clear as though in front of me
I wake up shaking, panicky
Flashes of images in my head,
Waking my slumber, sitting up in bed
Reliving each second, punishing thoughts,
Witnessing battles already fought

How did I make it this far?
So many voices from near and far
They overpower, fight and shout,
So much, it's hard to talk about
Existing, no life, a nightmare, a dream
Nothing's really here, nothing can be seen
Doors forever closed, no exit, no escape
Living with too much anger and hate.

A permanent fixture, present in everyone's world
Frozen in mine, standing in the cold.

Lost

Keep close, distance, stay away, how to handle each of them every
day
Exhausted, tired but never asleep, here not here, behaviour so deep
Try to keep safe, try to protect, all conversations all to deflect
I cannot think I cannot feel, where is the hope for any chance to
heal
Lost, lonely in this vessel, nothing left to give to this continuous
wrestle
Always alone for something I long, yet push them away before the
dawn

One mistake, and a burden since born
A lost life forever I'll mourn.

Home

Home is supposed to be a safe place
Home is where you belong, your own space
So why at home do I feel so alone?

Home is a place of care
Home is escape from judgemental stares
So why is home where I don't belong?

Home is a place to protect
Home is a place you don't feel bereft
So why is home where darkness springs from?

Home is full of love
Home is a place to return when you've had enough
So why is home a war zone?

Home is a place to feel complete
Home is a place never to feel weak
So why does home strip me to the bone?

Let go

Screw me now, let me go, no one ever needs to know
Let me leave, have my way, stop prolonging this nightmare day
Sleep, wake, each the same, nothing ever seems to change
The only thing that does remain, is me, the hatred, abuse and
blame
Hospital, medications, none have altered,
Community teams and therapy always faltered
So after weeks of playing these games, it's time to stop, bury the
hatchet and my name
I have tried, I really have, but things really are just too bad

So much to tackle for one small mind, I know it'll never all be fine
A constant struggle never to end, slight improvement but never on
the mend
I've had enough, it's time to leave, everyone's better off I firmly
believe
I'm stuck in an impossible place, nowhere to turn, no correction to
make
Every piece of work, each therapy, sinks me lower, drowning in
misery
It's all afresh, thoughts flash by, what did I do to deserve this, I
keep asking why?

But every question, its answer: worse, no strength to fight for life, no thirst

To keep struggling on this lonesome road, carrying an impossibly heavy load.

Too much to bear, for any woman, and nothing left to offer an empty helpless hand

So just be fair, let me go, to the inevitable end we all do know.

Abandoned

Everyone, everywhere always leaves,
Gives up, moves on, I'm left bereaved
To sit in my world with all I believe
Until I'm gone, and they won't even grieve

They'll all come round and finally see
This life, this journeys not meant to be
In my destruction they'll all be free
From problems passed blame and the shame of me

Lost, left with no hope or reprieve
Left bare, alone, like a distant dead tree
Choked by my past, and all its history
Suffocating slowly, unable to breathe

No way forward, no way to retrieve
A life now lost in painful memories
No chance to look back on what I've achieved
Or connect with those whose love I should receive

A choice is all I'd ask of you, if I could plead
But I've no energy left to change or vary

This cry for help no one will ever read
Someone to care, not give up is all I need

Or a rest from life, in death finally free
Except it's too much to ask, indeed
So lower the hatchet and with me bury
This body and mind who hurt so many

No chance of recovery, to succeed
No one to help, stuck with me
Trapped by life's appearances and greed
The runt of the litter, the bad seed

Darkness and depression is all I breathe
You ask where all of this can lead
Except in death no one will take heed,
A carcass on which others can feed.

My death, the end is an inevitability
All that's left is a body to bleed
A single teardrop, a tiny bead
Every failed attempt mocking me

So let me go; rip out root and weed
And burn it to ash, your final deed.

Hate

Hate me, berate me, shut me out
Speak harsh, speak fast, cruel words you spout
Blame me, shame me, shout all you like,
Lash out, crash out, scream with all your might.
Put me down, try to beat my resolve
Try to keep me in my place, but you've lost control
Cut off, shut off, say you don't care
Project, reject, I'll still be there
Punch me, hurt me, I'll still stay and stand
From this time on, I've the upper hand
Shout, scream, threaten to die
This time I won't listen to all your lies
Talk shit, rough, try to be tough
I've had enough of carrying your stuff
Accuse me of cheating, call me a slut, a whore
For this time, I leave,
I won't pass back through that door.

Slip

Deserted, forever hurt, left alone, locked up, flashbacks filth and
dirt
Lost, forever stuck, unable to escape from body and mind already
fucked
Voices, a reminder, a faceless man, no name
Mirrors no reflection, life's mental sick game
Body's own protection, at my skin I claw
One door, unable to shout from the floor
Another day, another test, so much blame, hatred, no chance of
rest
Start to relax, sudden flashback, unable to breathe, anxiety attack
Bleeding out, cuts so deep, never resting, insomniac, no sleep
Nights offer no relief, nothing but dreams, reality brief
Deeper I fall, reality slips, life's future hopes suddenly eclipsed.

Calories

Don't tell me I'm pretty, this I don't see
As in my reflection is all come to be
Calories and fats and numbers known
All in my appearance are constantly shown
Every roll and crease and unsightly fold
In my eyes I'm ugly to behold
Nothing worth looking at, nothing worth being
Just an apparition of what I've been eating

Agenda

Today's agenda, pamper session
A chance to relax and enjoy this blessing
Except I don't deserve a treat
For I am lost, helpless, pathetic, weak

Time to make, to keep myself and mind
Away from thoughts and criticism unkind
A cushion I make, of patchwork bits
Mismatched, uneven, they don't quite fit

They're like my life, scattered in strips
Nothing to believe in, but together I stitch
Begin to sew and hope for something new,
A wish for a life started anew

Creating something from disparate parts unknown
And there it sits complete, not perfect but something to own
To better, to tweak, it represents me
The scattered self, unable to be

Alone each bit is so separate,
Clinging to each strip so desperate

If only somehow there was a way
To rebuild me with stitches day by day

A needle and thread, a few hours passed,
Awake from slumber to start the task.
Except it's not all thread and cotton
To fit this self, so glib, forgotten

Scattered material, lying around
Trodden, walked over, hidden on the ground.

Relate

Feel my pain, feel it burn
This ever-present darkness at every turn
Feel it seethe and tear your soul
Dragging me down this endless road
A path of misery, a path of pain
A life so lost never regained
This hell-bent darkness, ever near
You the heart you truly fear
What is this life, suffering, misery?
Choking on smoke in this reverie
Feel my pain, feel it burn
Let it scorch and twist and yearn.

Pointless

Just another pointless day, wishing it were my last
Crafting, drawing, anything to distract, from the voices the flash
backs that I then react
I've hanged, been ill, cut and bled, the voices I'm trying to avoid fill
my head
Each day is harder, voices loud, fighting my care worker for support
somehow

No help is offered, you're on your own, to chase letters and notes,
hundreds of calls by phone
To struggle with daily suffering, when no hope of recovery,
treatment wears thin
Discharged from hospital without half my pills, working
relentlessly to fight with my will
Everything effort, no sleep, constant harm, not one moment of
calm

Ligature up the only reason I stopped, for getting it wrong,
hospital, living the nightmare plot
My escape plan in jeopardy, likely to fail, nowhere to run, help to
no avail

Where to begin to put stuff right, when each evening brings
flashbacks at night
And in the morning I wake to see, a person I don't recognise,
damaged, not slim, pretty me

One tight knot, a ligature, a belt, unable to breathe, an escape
from the path I'm dealt
Yet I remove it, back away, with a grain of hope for tomorrow,
however far away.

Control

Somehow, somewhere you lost it all
That last tiny grain of control
Ligatures tight until you're blue
Feeling that last air, disappear from you
But once more, you've been stopped again
By people who care, those heroic friends
But soon again you're left to your devices
And one deep cut, the hope you won't survive this
But time again, you're caught in the act
And your plans are evident, obvious in fact

Why to continue for people to try
To keep you safe, keep you alive
When nothing is better, life looks the same
And any recovery or therapy is at once in vain
Why can't you be left to take your life
If that's your wish, that should be your right
Not for someone to decide, to dictate
To hold the cards of your own fate

It doesn't seem fair, it's horrifyingly cruel
And only stubborn persistence does it fuel
That one day you'll finally succeed
And this life of yours, you'll no longer grieve.

Body

Constant worry, constant stress, body under such duress,
Pains and aches with every move, up and down, days never smooth
One minute coping, the next not, feeling like your confidence is
still shot
Exhausted, no reserves to cling to, just wanting my life back, feel
better soon
Everything seems to take so long, a broken record, stuck, skipping
on a song
No sleep to help bear the weight, no medication working to
compensate
Why so difficult, why so hard, my body, my skin, my soul is
scarred.

Hours

So many hours in a day
Only so many times you can say
I'm not coping, I'm really not okay
When nothing changes, day to day
When you feel you're repeating yourself
And chatting can never really help
And you spend hours each second
Chasing voices that constantly beckon
When each moment is a living nightmare
And you're a great pain, inconvenience to all who care
There's not enough in life to do
To distract, compensate, comfort you
Weeks go by to no end
No turn in the road, some fork, some bend
And so you stay on this potholed path
And await your fall and inevitable aftermath.

Disabled

Severely disabled but walking around
No wheelchair to illustrate what doctors have found
No sling or cast to show injury
No limping or staggering for people to see

A blank expression you always lend
Your worn mask of normality you defend
So the questions come and continue, at increasing rate
Why don't you work? How do you live?
Questions you hate

How to respond, to explain
Without showering them in your self-loathing rain
But they won't stop, no simple answer will do
No explanation sufficient, half-truths seen through

But if you say you bear the risk
Of being shunned, ignored, as they resist
Any contact with you and your 'problems'
Stuck again with no one to care, faith and trust fallen

No stranger, no person, no friend can ever truly understand

The stigma, the label, the difficulties of the damned
Wasting away in a world you don't seem to fit
So your illness does define and your soul submits.

Stranger

A stranger you say I've become
But you never knew me, not the real one
The Carla I hide deep within
The one exhausted, who's given in

You talk of plans and future dreams
To make me think positive by any means
How so, in a world of hurt, of pain and theft
You don't see, I've already gone, departed, left.

When your mind and soul have given in
There's nothing left but discomfort and sin
Just a shell of a person, a hollow twisted shape
Not carrying any hope for someone else's sake

A lost soul drifting, only existing
A mind beyond any prayer of fixing
A call, a cry for help to teams
Crisis there, for support, to lean

Yet not enough to give you any hope
No resolution in chats, just try to cope

It's all unbearable, sitting here with me
Even escaping my head to just to be

My insides are poisoned, dark and black
Constantly revisited, always under attack
What does it matter if I'm around?
And if I'm up there or in the ground?

So if I'm causing you so much pain
And I'm stuck, not changing, drowning in the rain
Then why fight for someone you've never met
A life, a path, a process already set.

Day

A difficult day, however you look, fighting trying but hope they
lack
Panic attacks and pain throughout the day, for what reason I
cannot say
Constant phone calls, chasing up, doing what my support work
should follow up

Yet here I am fighting away, desperately searching a future in some
way
To drag me out of this hell hole, where I am broken, a lost soul
But yet no one can help or take, any of this life, memories they've
made

Friends here so they say, yet never in an emotional support kind of
way
Always from a distance, never close, just enough to handle me in a
small dose
All so pointless, all this effort, that will never fix me, the broken
defect

Berated for swearing, yet mentally ill, but keep your manners,
social conventions still
It's all such bollocks, much baloney, leave me your stories away,
fuck off and let me be.

Plan

So now it's as simple as putting a plan in place
To end this pain, loathing and a life filled with hate
Death by drowning, head under water, a few short minutes
and body will falter
Why not suffocate, in this world I can't relate, just stop
breathing all pain leaving
Could cut deep until your blood seeps, draining this body,
Of all its worries, temporary pain for a lifetime of gain
I guess I could try a gun, that would be quick,
Just not so easy to acquire, too risky to misfire

So that leaves the old way, the one I dream of every day
The one I shouldn't have come back from
The one where night doesn't see dawn
No more screwing about with a mixture of pills, results in
doubt
Instead, hundreds of paracetamols, finally my escape
This time no stomach to bleed, no waking or giving people a
sense of need
Drive my car out of the way, and put an end to this everlasting
bad day

Go to sleep, maybe in pain, but still shit compared to this
constant rain
This I can look forward to, time to finish and start anew
Now just to bag them all, write all this up, settle my score.

Exit

So now it's done, once again I'm left
Feeling confused, undone, full of regret
Relationships reciprocal, dreams and flashbacks
Struggling, feeling so full, my life mapped
How on earth to carry on, searching for an exit
With so much going, my choice would be to just end it
It's all so dark and so bleak,
More to deal with every second
I have no energy to fight, too weak, lost all hope,
No help can beckon
I am leaving because they can do no more,
Tablets, psychology used to help
But I am here with the knowledge, lower than before,
Stuck with this hateful self,
Once I said, 'what's the difference in a day'
If I die tomorrow, a month, a week, today
At least I won't have to listen to the voices
Just endless sleep.

Crack

A hair-thin crack, hidden like a rancid lie
It's a shadow somewhere behind the eyes
A haunting, desperate, choking fog
Of past memories and times people forgot
But it lingers there, something stalking inside
That demonic vision yet trying to hide
A single scratch, ever present ahead
Still fluorescent and blinding behind closed lids
The sadistic cut of every scar
The masochistic beatings of a honing radar
They're all a sign of something unseen
Something lived and yet never-ending dream
The damage is left, the debris dark
The piercing reality of a barren life, stark.

Help

Don't mind us, we're here to help
Get you back to your good old self
Don't worry, don't panic, it'll all be fine
They can't see the horror, they're blind
Breathe, don't panic, take a deep breath
I can't, I won't, I've got nothing left
In through your nose, out through your mouth
Stop being critical, filling yourself with doubt
You need to cry, need that release
But I can't let out this inner beast
It's all too much, too much to bear,
The voices they hound, they berate, they scare
They say it all like it's so simple
But it's a part of you like a little dimple
Ever present, ever marked
You're fighting a war
Alone
In the Dark.

Admission

No change of meds, we don't want you here that long
But community teams can do that when you've gone
It's just because you'll feel more suicidal
And, therefore, if we adjust you'll be here a while
So better to make changes when you're at home
In the place you said you came in from
The same spot from which you came committed
And tried to kill yourself, had you been permitted
So we'll let you go back to lack of support
To isolation, alone, no nursing staff rapport
To help you through the changes ahead
And have your room empty, a spare bed
Just so you don't get stuck, institutionalised
And no one will hear your heart-wrenched cries
We honestly feel it's for the best
That for your two-week stay and rest
We change nothing to help you cope
And therefore give no semblance of hope
To make sure when you're discharged
You go back and maintain our caring façade
Of concern for your welfare with heartless stares
And empty words in high-seated chairs
And you'll return whence you came
To start this process all over again.

Pens

What do they think, when they sit with their pens
Their briefcases and note-book friends,
Sneering above their glasses, poised on the tip of their nose
Staring with a wry grin as your anxiety grows
They sort and flick through page after page
Every note, assessment, your life at every stage
All sat in a row, a seated firing squad
Intimidating you to communicate in nods

Those blank faces, all bored and unimpressed
They who seem comfortable in your evident distress
Those strangers with their clipped tongues and squinty eyes
Are the people who will finally decide
Who you are, what you have
Where you've been, and who you've seen
Your medication, story, and future plans
Ready to discharge you with a flick of their hands

For an hour's quick glance, barest facts
With no consolation or assistance given back
Left open, vulnerable at a nameless face
A life you've lived, torn out displaced

And there you sit, attempt to talk it through
With the trauma, abuse, all perfectly true
A life story, your existence, your being,
Hoping your reality is what they're seeing

To hope when you've finished crying your tears
You won't be left with your ultimate fear
Four blank faces staring back at you
As though what you've said is old and untrue
That compassion, help, care for others
Will suddenly open to this stark world only you discover
You came for help, for quiet, a hand
And left with judgements all written in sand.

File

What's in that file over there?
The one labelled me and all of my care
That people constantly refer to
And add bits and pieces all about you
Why can't I ever take a look?
At my life story, this mental health book
If I'm the protagonist, then surely I know
Each and every page as though I wrote it on my own?

Except it's composed by hundreds of names
None of which to me bear a claim
Except perhaps some passing acquaintance at some time
And then they make decisions about this life of mine
How can so much have been said
About this life I've never read?
A bystander in my own epoch
A world of opinion all locked up

What could it all possibly say?
A liar, cheat, fraud in some way?
Dangerous, manipulative, sociopathic, at risk
Psychotic, depressed, a failure, an endless list?

How can it be that those faces know
So much more than I can ever show?
I've got my words, my experience, my pain
They've got evidence that will always remain
Just black marks, letters, on sheets of paper
So why the concealment, the evasion, always "later"

Am I that ill that I just can't know?
Living some fairy Truman-like show
Am I beyond help or repair
The truth I'll be like this forever, the scare?
Am I that far gone I believe I'm mad
When really there isn't anything rotting, bad
But somehow I've convinced myself I'm like this
Signed my own sections with a smile or a kiss?

Request it all they say, though it'll take months
But then it'd be here, in its entirety, this lump
And would I care to look inside
Uncover some truth they've tried to hide
And then to be left with the knowledge, never to depart
Leaving a sinking, deadening feeling in my heart
Would it all be the final straw
My life strewn out all over the floor?

Relax

Sit, drink tea, it'll make you feel better, you'll see
You'll soon be out and about and all of this will sort itself out
Don't stress, sit back, just relax, we've been doing this, years going
back
You're in the right place, we'll take care of you
There's nothing that we can't do for you
Just think, in here at least you're safe
We'll keep reviewing things, you, looking at your case
It's okay, you can't help how you feel
You've had a hard life, a rotten deal
You don't deserve what's happened to you
And you will get through this, you will pull through
I know you've said that time and again
But still we'll ask, how can we get you on the mend
There's always a way through, just give it time
So it might take years, who cares, its fine
You're still young, you'll bounce back from
Everything that's happened, just stay strong.

Visits

How are you? Silly question I know
It's just so hard to know what to say
When you're in such a bad way
How's your sleep, are you getting some rest?
You're really not looking at your best
You look drawn out, you need a break
I wish the pain away I could take

Oh don't cry, I'm sure it'll get better
Give it a few weeks, change in the weather
Are you getting out, bit of fresh air?
Take a long walk, forget your cares
How are you eating, are you having enough?
See that'll help all your mental health and stuff
What about exercise, that's supposed to be good
Positive endorphins that all should –

Don't you want to be well?
Why are you isolating yourself in a cell?
You're not trying to help yourself
You need to look after your health
Have you heard from family? I know they text

I'll let them know things, briefly at best
You know they care, want to be in touch,
Everyone's just so busy and such

Friends, what about any of them?
Well, I'm sure love and support they send
People just don't know what to say
How to relate to you each day
You need to make more effort on your part
Keep in touch, message them, make a start
Or you will lose people, you'll be alone
In this dark hole you've decided to make home.

If you just tried a little harder
You're a clever girl, be smarter
I'm not accusing you, I'm trying to help
Help us see what you've done to yourself
Pull yourself together, keep your chin up
Drop all this nonsense crying and stuff
Be thankful for the roof over your head
And the opportunities you've had, experiences you've led.

Well I guess I'd best get on my way
I've one hell of a manic day
Got a party of people coming around
So much to prepare I can't hang around
If you need me, you know where we are
Only on the end of a phone like before.
Except I might be busy, not sure with everything's going on
But if I get a missed call I'll see who it's from

I'll message you back when I can
But my life goes on, doesn't stop and stand.

Anyway, love you, speak to you soon, I'll try to catch you in a week
or two
When life's calmed down I'll check in on you.

Cackling

No it's fine, I love wasting hours
With nothing to do, no talk, no power
No ability to leave although informal
Because I'm a risk, not well enough for normal.

Its great fun stuck in rooms and locked corridors
Walking around staring at the floor
Hoping it might open and swallow you up
Or someone might show they give a fuck.

I love being asked thirty times a day
If I'm alright, if everything's okay
With no waiting for the answer
Just shuffling past a little faster.

I think it's great to overhear
That your weekend is finally nearly here
Of all your plans and what you're up to
When I'll still be here, same walls, same view.

I look forward to your cackling laughter
Travelling from the staff room, after

A patient's done something so very funny
At least their pain made your day sunny.

I lie in wait for the endless empty chat
Of help and care plans and all that
With the same questions and numbing response
And your enthusiasm, looks, nonchalance.

It's great to hear midnight alarms
Of patients trying to do themselves harm
Seeing the same pain-stricken face
And the screams that echo, compete and chase.

I'm really grateful to be on the ward
With no clothes or make up, possessions or cords
To sit and stare at the obvious suffering
Written as though it's therapeutic and comforting.

To surround yourself with people as ill as you
Or those not quite so but will be soon
I am really glad you're keeping me safe
To remain a vegetable and leave in this same state.

I feel so lucky to be alive
I mean, in here, why would anyone want to die?

Taboo

How to talk about a subject so taboo
Yet everywhere it surrounds you
Beneath the smiling draped veneer
The paper-thin cracks start to appear
When everyone's life is such a show
Of how well they're doing for all to know
But yet not quite capturing the truth
The ones that run deeper with even stronger roots
We've created a reality of make-believe
Where no one's happy and no one is free
All sorted by an evening with a snap of a glass of wine
Where everything is smiles, always fine
But what of those you don't see
No repetitive posts or likes for me
The ones you don't notice in the street
Head down, shuffling, surrendered defeat
The people you'll never really get to meet
Those who go home alone
Who are hounded by a never-ending drone
And so exist without a life
And will disappear into the darkness, with no bright lights
Sometimes we're so blind to see
The reality we've carved out in our society.

Repeat

It's only a day and today is a day in its entirety, no way of
repeating, however defeating
The past cannot replicate, life is renewed with each deep sleep
But memories will always resonate and feel as though this
repetition is your fate
The pain isn't there but the feelings remain, you relive your trauma
and you're left with regret
With the feeling of self-sustain, there's no way to undo everything
you've suffered, all that was done to you

They say time is the greatest healer, and yet you're left with
something deeper
A dark, torn, drawn out scar that will never fade, however long
ago, however far
But today is not that day, it cannot for all your fear recur
And yet those feelings you cannot defer, they may be re-
experienced in sudden flashes
Your past colliding in overwhelming clashes
But today is only one day and can never be done,
Different day, different month, another year redone.

Informal

Hospital, as you may have guessed, is my new location, my new
address
With twenty women, with staff who walk by without care
With no safe place to hide away, no one to witness the voices that
say
To hurt, to harm, finally to give up, their only clue, a lacerated cut
More unsettled than ever before, an empty room, a bed, a floor
Harassed by voices, visions that stare, the constant noise, trying to
ensnare
Stuck, distressed, nowhere to turn, my only companion, locked
away, I yearn
The only comfort, my complete demise, the quiet from the voices
trying to pry
Cut off, incarcerated without a phone, no connection to the world
in this dead zone
Trapped and left with a person, left to see, my greatest enemy, my
detested me.

Pop

Pop and take another pill
Lose yourself further your will
To make your decisions for yourself
To look after yourself, your body, your health
Do as they continue to say
Bend yourself to their judgements and way
Don't be yourself, be a follower true
Forget the person at the centre, you
Just become a little robot
Someone able to fit in their box.

Review

Doctors don't understand me, with my disassociation, and
emotional dysregulation.
They see me sitting all composed, and then, presume that they
know
That I have the capacity to care what happens to me when people
aren't there
They don't understand; it's the psychosis that makes me hurt
myself, and get me into self-harming hell
They think it's all straightforward, and I feel like I'm being ignored
Changing all my prescribed medication to PRN isn't helping my
head
They don't understand that I can't take responsibility to not be out
and to be free
To hurt myself and finish my life and put an end to struggle and
strife
So how to communicate to them, all that I say but never
comprehend
How much of a struggle every day I have to fight, to let voices not
get their own way
It's too much to fight on so many fronts, too much for one person
to confront

With voices, bulimia, personality disorder, to be able to see a future
past PTSD, go forward
A section would relieve some pressure, which I know would be
measured
In my acceptance of feeling more safe and the responsibility
someone else could take
My care-co and nurse, I know, won't help, except to say I'm trying
to protect myself
However hard that may be and when no recovery can I see
I feel a sense of loss, already of the day being so unsteady
With no clue of the outcome of the meeting, no sense of resolution,
with lack of sleeping
It could take weeks to stabilise meds, right, and in that time,
somehow, I've got to fight
I'm exhausted, I don't have the energy or the capacity actually to
see
A way out of this mess that is my world, and so I'm left vulnerable,
totally exposed
With some miracle I'll find a way to be able to recover, fully to stay
Until I feel safe with myself and continue, to get some real genuine
help
That or I'll be back in A & E, dead or to repeat the process, not
unlock a vital key
And maybe start finally to feel in control of my fucked-up
psychotic little world
Away from hounding and hallucinations, to a society I am welcome
I've literally done all I can but I take a logical stance, I'm begging
for a break, a chance
But tomorrow will be a pointless meeting and I won't be able to
resolve what I'm seeking
Oh, to have it all sorted, over, done, and in my death, accept I've
finally won.

Course

Go to a course, sit in a room, with staring strangers, surrounding
that loom
To talk about feelings, compassion and such and all can think, who
gives a fuck?
Practise mindfulness, try to be present, how can I be when it's all so
unpleasant
My past is gruelling, my future not there, and I'm supposed to sit
and start to care
To try to be nice to myself, all about that hippy self help
And yet, however hard I try, I look at the years, the days gone by
The minutes, the hours of my day and can only think with great
dismay
There's no resolution, no recovery for me, this side I'll return to, it's
all just me
I am screwed up, I am a product of my past, life passing me by so
fucking fast
In the same position just a year ago and I'm the expert on me, I
should know
That really hope is truly lost, and one day my life will be the cost.

Future

Trying to focus on a future, whilst I sit with my neck sutured
From the demons that scream aloud, the constant drone of a
bustling crowd
Demands of harm and suffering still, trying to disrupt, break my
will
As I fight the constant ache, of a life I wish to take, forsake
I read of courses of recovery but with this comes a wrenching
discovery
I can't picture a way forward, to try new treatments, to get on
board
When every reflection I sickeningly loathe, this being of mine I'm
perpetually betrothed
To a life of misery and strife, which could all be mended with one
sharp knife
If only people could understand my distress, my life in tatters, my
mind a mess
With constant chatter from those not there, the knowing sense that
nobody cares
Can't understand the pressure, the torment, and so I sit stuck in
this life dormant
Unable to free myself from anguish, my only expression in
emotionless language

No drive to carry on fighting ahead, no rest at night for flashbacks
in bed
No seeming hope to pull through, where every voice haunts,
destroys you
Can I really have some parallel world, where I am well, my
sentence served?
Finally free from this conveyor belt, finally safe with my thoughts,
my self
Oh, to wish for the will to carry on, to be part of this society I don't
belong
To accomplish something, to become, a person, coping, living,
finally won.

Back

Back home alone for so long,
Afraid, anxious, it could all go so wrong
So many hours, so much time
To argue and fill this life of mine
With jobs and lists and never-ending tasks
And so many questions to care teams to ask
Weeks full of doctors, appointments, meds
Trying to remember all that's been said
Visitors too, by the handful
Making sure you're okay, so thankful
That 'you're back in your little home'
Not getting from your responses or tone
That you're still struggling
That despite how you seem, each minute is punishing
Of the normal, recovered; reset and restart
It's part of your condition to play the part

But here's the thing, it's the time in-between
When no one's around, your downtime unseen
When you're needing a cry but not weepy
Ever exhausted, tired not sleepy
When you need to vent some frustration

Relieve the ever-building tension
When you've sorted and cleaned, done all you can
Tried to read, written, followed 'coping strategies plan'

That you realise how unwell you are still
And that black abyss is your life, always ill.

Tackle

Trying to tackle something so large, when you don't feel you've
been in charge
Of what happened to you, all your history, of your world, your
individual story
How can someone sit and explain, just to be positive from all your
pain
When they don't, can't understand, you're the way you are by
other people's hands
In yourself, your being, figuratively, and in your trauma, quite
literally
I guess only time can ever tell, if you can move on, not dwell in this
hell
On every experience you've had, away, to keep those knocking
doors at bay
Somewhere, somehow, you'll find a focus, not have those past
ghosts continually choke us
To beat them finally to be on point, and not constantly upset those
you feel you disappoint
Cut out those who really upset, gain some distance and self-love
and respect
So as not to repeat every day, like some sort of never-ending
byway.

Shout

Concentrate, argue, shout if you can
Make a future, some goals, some plan
Even to get through each day
Keep safe, and sustain, come what may
So much easier said than done
But I will fight, I will finally have won
Just three positives, just three a day
However dark or dreary, simplistic some might say
But what if it helps, helps you to see
That every day isn't as bad as it feels or could be
Even if I have to deal with voices
Daily, still in life I'll have choices
It may be in cycles, may happen again
But life's not about the storm
It's about me dancing in the rain.

Hard

I never thought it would be this hard, where everywhere I look
there's, plastic, glass shards
To try to quit self-harm behaviours and stop destructive self-
thoughts of failure
When actually in stopping you're keeping yourself safe, even if
that's not the phrase
That you ever really want to hear, when you're so close to the edge
you feel it here
In your heart and with voices all around, every bang, shout, every
loud sound
When all you want is some pain, to concentrate, ground, release
And drain you of those voices and feelings for a minute, instead
you're having to learn and sit
With how you are and what you're worrying about, and not let
anything throw recovery into doubt
But it's more difficult than I ever thought, even if it's the future
I've always sought
To be well, happy, settled and secure, not plagued by demons that
constantly lure
You into patterns you don't want to repeat, and yet you can't find
the solace that you seek.

Six days past, my anxiety is unbearable, my mood shifts hardly
variable
Except this constant incessant need, to hurt myself deeply, to
watch and bleed
It almost becomes an obsession, when voices don't give you a break
and beckon
Not a habit, not as easily solved, but part of your core from years of
trauma now old
If I could have just one wish, it'd be to end this nightmare quick
And just be normal, like everyone else, suffering with life's normal
worry and self.

Admission

It can be hard to admit you've had an all right day
Like you're a fraud for being okay in some way
To see the small positives, glimpses of light
That the whole day hasn't been a constant fight

But those moments must be cherished, recognised
Greeted with thankful, heart-warming surprise
Because they offer some guiding hope
To know for some time, you're able to cope

That not all is darkness and simply pain
That those feelings have in some way waned
Just for a minute or pleasing hour
You've had some calm, some sense of power

To change the way that you've been feeling
Give your life some purpose, some meaning
They may be small, they may seem trivial
But they are the seconds that make like liveable.

Faith

I'm not religious yet in faith
I find so much I can relate
To being kind, honest, open-hearted and true
In being freed from bondage in faith through you

That depression is a sickness in the name
And focusing keeps life lived in vain
More a belief in the supernatural
Turn your life into love not factual

You are special, you are you,
That cannot be replicated or renewed
A singular person so unique
Thoughts of voice, powerful to speak

Find in faith a mustard grain
Find the strength to sustain
And one day it'll grow into a mountain
And you can drink from life's glorious fountain

Of fun and family, friends and belief
And in your faith, you'll find the relief you desperately seek.

Kin

It really is the strangest thing,
Where you meet your kind, your kin
In a society that shuts you away
Hides your illness in judgement and dismay
But in the darkness of those places
The safe and hidden spaces
Suddenly you find a whole new spot
Where everyone is similar, that discarded side-lined 'lot'

Yes, all are ill to varying degrees
Some more easily diagnosed to see
But despite their labels, they're just people too
And suddenly you feel you belong, true
A group of misfits cast together
With no preconceptions of one another
Just acceptance that we're somehow alike
In our personal battles and strife

Whether our history is much the same
Or we're given the same pigeonholed name
There's a whole range of suffering and age
Someone always on the same page

The same diagnosis, meds and symptoms
Instant friendships without the distance.
Someone to truly relate to
Who understands and feels your point of view

Every hospital, refuge, respite stay
I find myself navigating to a face in some way
Towards someone I don't know
Wanting to reach out and say hello
And suddenly you're no longer alone
You're stood with people unknown
Two souls lost however cruel
There is a deep earthy pull

You start to unite with personal fight
And spend your time soul-searching day and night
You suddenly realise the mental health taboo
Is only constructed, perpetuated by the likes of you
That those that suffer are the most compassionate
With lives and experiences that truly fascinate
How, in the words of the criminally and mentally insane,
There's someone like you, same heart, same brain.

Bound together, forever these souls won't part
Maybe a while in distance, but never in mind or heart.

Overwhelmed

Sometimes you feel overwhelmed and tearful
Full of stress and constantly fearful
Of what you have and what you worry you'll lose
Of pain and hurt and more than one bruise
You cannot change how you feel
And deep wounds inside are hard to heal
That or you feel dead inside
And every day you do your best to hide
From everyone's criticism, judgements and questions
As though you're making slow success
It's not always at another's rate, at best
Sometimes it's just a poison within
And you feel completely like giving in
It's all too hard to explain
To anyone about trauma and pain
It's okay to have a bad day and wallow
To get through each minute of the day's hollow
But try to see the beauty in tomorrow anew,
New start, new chance, the total new you.

Strength

Somewhere within you've the strength
To tackle the problems you've had a length
To fight and finally start to succeed
And live the life you long to lead

To move on, rebuild and recover
That sense of you finally to discover
The one who's not just mentally ill
But is determined with iron will
To become the person they now wish to be
Finally to set themselves truly free

It may be hidden, it may take courage
But you will be able to prosper and flourish
One day something will suddenly change
And life will start to re-arrange
And nothing will be quite so bleak
Some sense of refuge you desperately seek
For things cannot remain the same
Life is given after the rain.

A tiny bud of hope, a sprout,

After a long, unrelenting drought
So take solace in the fact
You've the will to fight back.

Be strong, be bold and be brave
Remember this each and every day.

Partner

A partner is a powerful thing
To share and be open about all you've seen
To be loved and respected for all you are
Even haunted by demons, not so far
To be able to be accepted and totally honest
Loved for all your anguish, at worst or best
Suddenly you realise in your soul
A mate for life felt, a love so old
Like days of courting in times gone by
A shadow so big, an umbrella so high
A tree with hardy steady roots
That will grow and flourish and shoot
To grow stronger each week, each day
And blossom each year, a beautiful array
Of colours, leaves, blossom all around
Together we will remain always bound.

Flaws

When you realise someone isn't perfect
It's easy to focus on their defects
The harder choice is to accept that life
Won't always be how it's meant
That it throws trouble and difficulties your way
And you fight on each and every day
Everyone knows things are not so great
But some are harder to swallow with life mistakes,
Things can be managed as best we can
Then grow into a helping hand
The relationship will have many challenges
Some may leave you totally astounded,

But judgements do not help you or them
And you have to accept your strengths aren't the same
They're not perfect but none of us are
And what they offer is better than nice houses or cars
Of bad health or money or infatuated love
They offer support and care more than enough
Any challenge faced can be overcome
If you want for a future, you can have one
Situations change and life gets harder

But you've got to have some sort of starter
A willingness to change and compromise too
And your life will be happy with life renewed.

Baggage

When you meet someone, there is always an issue
Ex-partners, money, alcohol, drug misuse
Everyone has baggage, everyone has a past
Some easier to solve, some that leave scars
But the most important things to remember
It won't always be like that forever
If that person touches your soul
You feel that pull, that connection, feelings of old
When they make your heart miss a beat
They are the one you hang on to and keep
Relationships are hard, challenges for all
But if in love you deeply fall
Anything can be overcome, a past rewritten
You'll find a way through smiles both smitten,
And you can have an amazing life
Together, forever as man and wife.

Scale

It's only a number on a scale
Not worth hurting or trying to impale
Yourself over something oh so small
Setting yourself up for a greater fall
Every time you step and a figure you see
Not a true reflection of all that you be
And yet it soon becomes all you are
And you look at yourself from afar
You stare and hone on each little detail
And let your emotions run off the rails
It's time to take a step further back
And drop the I'm-not-good-enough act
And accept that you're more than a shape
And your life is worth more than the calories you take
Try to see the you that's inside
The one that tries to cower and hide
And see the person the world does witness
Not defined by your weight or fitness
But that you're healthy
That you're true
You're a person
Lovely
You're you.

Rest

A second's rest is all it takes
A brief escape from self-loathing, hate
To remind you that you are worth more
Than what you've allowed yourself before
That you are worthy and deserving
That your life is worth preserving
That somewhere you're honest and true
Your soul not marred by what you've been through

You are not defined simply by your past
And you've got a new purpose, a task
To be kinder to yourself for a second
See the person others do beckon
Out from the darkness and into the light
A future you, just in sight.

Movement

Sometimes things just start to happen and everything falls into
place
Support worker, help, assistance and the like, and you're not
making fifty phone calls to chase
When you get a care-co which does its job, keeps you updated and
in the loop
Takes the stress away with one call, no more jumping through
mental health hoops
When you finally see the care-in co-ordinator, and start to feel
they're at your back, supporting
People around you start to understand and listen, and everything's
written down, accurately reporting
It's nice to finally feel things are moving forward, not getting
stuck,
Maybe this time it'll happen and I'll stay well, and continue to
progress out of this continuous ravine and rut.

Name

Even writing today's date, seems a little bizarre to take
I truly believed I wouldn't make it this far,
And to be fair, I tried pretty hard
And yet here I sit in the garden with bird song,
Looking at myself, how far I've come
And here today brings a new thought
Not just not but something I often thought
Knowing my name holds so much negativity
To past, to pain, a life of captivity

So I began to start to ask myself
Three questions that have always helped
You reflect on the good times in a year
Not dwelling on the bad, but on the cheer
What is your best memory?
Meeting those this year that believed in me
What is your biggest achievement?
Surviving the year, asking for help and treatment
What is your hope throughout the year?
To continue to discover me, take charge and steer

To a life I want, where I feel I belong

Ceasing the depression that too long prolonged
I've already started to rebuild me
And a future I finally have to see
With someone I like, someone I can love
That old Carla I'm past, bored of
Time to reinvent, discovery for myself
Not to be limited by roles, silenced and shelved

And so I may not have written, but I've pondered a while
Returning to those thoughts, I began to smile
My gut responded, a definitive sign
That you're thinking on the right lines
What better way to claim myself, this new life
Than to change my surname, cut old ties with a knife
A family name, that causes nothing but pain
A link to the past that shall always remain
Why carry the presence of my struggles?
Remain living with the cloud of a mental health bubble

If I am truly to reinvent me,
What a way to start afresh and free
A little bit of research into my name,
All are French, all origins the same
Carla means free woman, who stands tall,
Strength in herself makes sure she doesn't fall
Daniel(le) defeated a den of lions which made me smile
It's reminiscent of my life and living style
Bridget stands for power and strength
Something I've had to find at length

So now the surname is all that's left
To change and reclaim, a decision I won't regret
Something with meaning, and now French roots
From which I can empower and grow new shoots
I looked at rebirth, strength and resilience
But needed to find something unique and different
A passing comment, an insight said
There's a warrior in you Carla, who's fought that head
And there it was, just one search later
As soon as I saw it, I knew it was a taker
Carla Danielle Bridget Baudin
It even sounds as though it goes hand in hand

Reflects my deep and sensitive side
And it's a name in which I can now take pride
It works, it fits, its meaning is true
A free-woman, fighting, a warrior through and through
A name never to change or forget
To hold on to and never regret
A name that defines my new chapter in life
Not linked to past memories or disliked
My new name shall be my light to remind me on dark dreary
nights

I am not the girl I used to be,
I am Carla Baudin, a fighter, I'm me.

Change

How to make yourself anew
With everything you've been through
All you've seen and all you've felt
All the hands that you've been dealt

Try to envisage a new you
Someone you'd like to grow into
When you're stuck with a past that never goes away
It's time to try a different way

So change it, choose, mix things up
Break the cycle in which you're stuck
Discover all of life's fine intricacies
Find a route, be proud, be pleased

One quick piece of paper
And then a short ten days later
There you are: new name, reborn
Not to be traced, never to feel torn

Between the old you and family name
But now to accept yourself again
Find the means to be strong and free
A person to become, finally just me.

Finale

I never believed it could happen, it's true
Life could turn around out of the blue
That one event could be so huge
And give you a break, a new sense of refuge
From all you've been through and all you've felt
Suddenly a change in the hand you've been dealt
And suddenly life's less harassing than before
Offering a sense of purpose ever more
For me a pregnancy quite unexpected
That left those feelings of life rejected
No more prevalent in my mind
Just a sense of hope, a sign
Then with one opportunity came another
Not just the chance to be a mother
But a new home, a future, an aim
Life would never look quite the same
Suddenly all experiences past
Became just that, never more my task
To manage and handle and constantly seek
A new way to be from everything so bleak
Now a life I can truly see
Now anew I can finally be

No more medication, no more fear
Just calm and happiness and a baby so dear
A new perspective, a new outlook
A chapter in my life, closed, encapsulated in this book.

Voices

Through the Dark

Carla Baudin's next project is a verbatim poetry book entitled, *Voices Through the Dark*. The poetry hopes to encapsulate the multifaceted nature of recovery, and stories that will move and bring a positive and more hopeful outlook to the reader. They will be positive in tone, hoping to bring a sense of achievement and hope to the reader that recovery is something achieved by many, and is therefore possible for anyone.

The poetry may include parts of the very personal journey through mental health, thoughts and aspects of the mental health system, aids for recovery as well as some details about the subject as a person. It will remain completely anonymous except to use the first name as the title of the poem. If you would like to use a pseudonym then you are welcome to.

If you would like to be included in this project, or know someone who would, then please email Carla directly at baudin.carla@outlook.com to receive a form.